Where the Waves Break
Life at the Edge of the Sea

Where the Waves Break
Life at the Edge of the Sea

by Anita Malnig

photographs by

Jeff Rotman, Alex Kerstitch, and Franklin H. Barnwell

A Carolrhoda Nature Watch Book

Carolrhoda Books, Inc./Minneapolis

*For my parents, Lawrence and Laura Malnig,
who introduced me to the sea*

Consulting Editor: Franklin H. Barnwell,
Associate Professor, Department of Ecology
and Behavioral Biology, University of
Minnesota

*The photograph of the beached jellyfish on page 41
is used through the courtesy of Lola Beall Graham.*

Additional photo credits can be found on page 48.

A note on scientific classification can be found on page 45.

Manufactured in the United States of America.

This book is available in two editions:
Library binding by Carolrhoda Books, Inc.
Soft cover by First Avenue Editions
241 First Avenue North
Minneapolis, Minnesota 55401

LIBRARY OF CONGRESS CATALOGING IN PUBLICATION DATA

Malnig, Anita.
   Where the waves break.

      "A Carolrhoda nature watch book."
      Includes index.
      Summary: Examines the various marine animals and
   plants found along the edge of the sea.
      1. Seashore biology—Juvenile literature.
   [1. Seashore biology] I. Title. II. Series.
   QH95.7.M347   1984   574.5′2638   84-9614
   ISBN 0-87614-226-9 (lib. bdg.)
   ISBN 0-87614-477-6 (pbk.)

      5   6   7   8   9   10   93   92   91   90   89

The edge of the sea is a curious place. Whether the coastline is rocky or sandy, life at the seashore brews and bubbles, but seeing it often takes a sharp eye. Whole neighborhoods of sea creatures may live under the rocks or burrowed in the sand. Some sneak out for food at night, dodging larger animals. Others never leave their damp, dark hiding places. Still other animals are in disguise, looking more like plants than animals. The closer you look, the more you will see.

5

High tide on a Long Island, N.Y., beach

If you go to the beach at different times of the day, you will notice that the shore looks different. Sometimes the water comes far up on the shore, covering rocks and beach. This is called high tide. At other times you can walk far out on the beach, over the area that was covered by water during high tide. This is low tide. Low tide is a good time to look for shells and rocks or for animals that live in the sand.

The moon has a lot to do with these high and low tides. Like the earth, the moon has a gravitational pull. The moon's gravitational pull makes the water that is nearest to the moon rise up. The water on the opposite side of the earth also piles up higher, but this

Low tide on the same beach

rise is caused largely by the rotation, or spinning, of the earth. This means that two places are always having a high tide at the same time. And two other places are having a low tide at the same time.

Low tide comes 6 hours and about 13 minutes after high tide. Then the day's second high tide comes, 12 hours and 25 minutes after the first. The follow-ing day the two high tides and the two low tides will happen 50 minutes later than they had the day before.

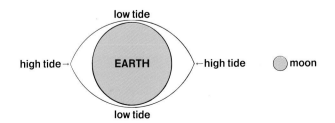

7

During low tide we can wander far out along the beach and see plants and animals that at another time might be under water. One very good place to look is in a tide pool. A tide pool is just that—a small pool filled with ocean water that was left behind when the tide went out. You'll find these pools mostly on rocky coasts where the rocks make holes that collect the water.

Each pool is its own little community. Sea creatures you find in one may not be in another. Tide pool life varies according to location and climate as well. You would not expect to find exactly the same animals in a New England tide pool as you would in a Mediterranean one. Some kinds of tide pool creatures exist almost anywhere in the world—starfish, sponges, and mussels, to name just a few—even though their colors, sizes, and shapes may vary from place to place.

Sometimes during low tide the pools dry out a little. This can be a problem for the creatures living there. Some hide from the sun under rocks where it is damp and dark. Others hide in clumps of seaweed.

One animal you're very likely to find in or around a tide pool is the snail. There are about 40,000 different kinds of saltwater snails, and there are many others that live in fresh water or on land.

Snails often look as if they are slowly sliding along, but they are using their feet to get around. A snail has one muscular foot. The snail squeezes its foot muscles together, then lets them go, inching along bit by bit.

Some snails use their feet as shovels. A tiny digging action moves what is in the snail's path and helps it go forward. Burrowing—digging a tunnel and then using it for shelter—comes in handy if a snail needs to escape from another animal, like a starfish. There is even one kind of snail, called a harp shell, that can use its foot to trick animals wanting to capture it. This snail is able to break off the back part of its foot. That broken-off part remains wriggling in the sand, sure to attract the attention of the attacking animal. Meanwhile, the rest of the snail can sneak off.

Snails also have one or two pairs of tentacles that help them sense danger. On one pair, often at the tips, are eye-spots, which are sensitive to light.

The underside of a snail showing its broad foot. The tube between the snail's tentacles is called the proboscis. The snail's mouth is located here.

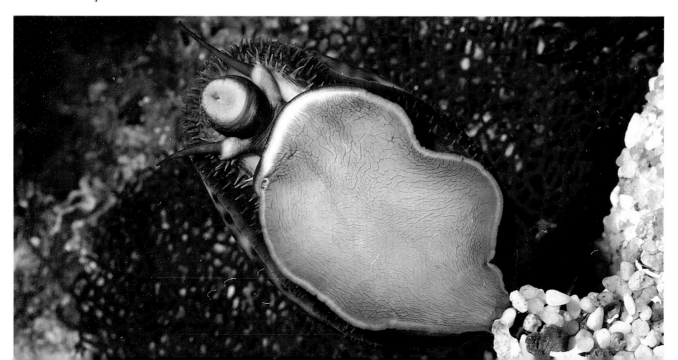

In this picture of a helmet shell snail, the foot, tentacles, and one eyespot can be clearly seen.

A moon snail eating a sand dollar. The fleshy mass at the base of the snail is an enlargement of the front part of its foot, called the propodium. The expanded foot helps the snail to plow through the sand and to hold its food.

Extending from the front (right) of this fingerprint snail is its siphon.
Water is drawn over the snail's gill through the siphon. The gill takes oxygen
from this water so that the snail can breathe. These snails and some others are
able to extend a brightly colored fold of tissue, called the mantle, over their shells.

Brightly colored turban shell snails like this one
are usually found in warmer waters. They feed on
algae.

A small Gulf of California snail, called a trivia,
creeping over a colony of coral

You'll find snails in ocean waters all over the world. Adult snails range in length from .04 inch (1 mm) to 2 feet (60 cm) or more. These 2-foot-long snails live in waters around Australia.

The longest snail of all is almost 52 inches (132 cm) long and makes itself at home in the body of a sea cucumber. Though unusually long, this snail is only .2 inch (5 mm) in diameter.

Periwinkles are found all over the world. This one (left) is shown next to a New England moon snail.

The periwinkle, a common tide pool snail, is easy to find. Periwinkles cluster together by the hundreds on rocks, many in cracks and crevices. A filmy layer of algae, a kind of sea plant, covers the rocks, but you may not be able to see it. Using teeth too small to see, the periwinkle grazes this plant for its daily food.

As many as 860 million periwinkles can live along just one mile of rocky coast. Together in one year they can eat about 2,200 tons of material, but only 55 tons is food they can digest. The rest is the rock they scraped off along with the algae!

Another animal commonly found in tide pools is the starfish. The starfish gets its name because its arms, also called rays, often make it look like a star. Along those arms the starfish has little tube feet tipped with suction cups. These can grasp rocks tightly and are used by the starfish to move around. At the end of each arm is a sensitive eyespot. This eyespot cannot see things, but it can tell light from dark.

The small, whitish "pebbles" beneath the starfish, periwinkles, and crab in this tide pool are actually animals called barnacles.

A starfish feeding on a crab. The arrow points to an eyespot. The "hairs" on the upper right arm are the starfish's extended tube feet.

14

*Although most kinds of starfish have five arms, sun stars,
such as this one seen from beneath, have more.*

*A close-up of the suction cups at the ends of a starfish's tube feet. In this
picture the tube feet are not extended. They can be retracted even further
and the red spines around them will cover and protect them.*

A starfish opening a mussel with sea urchins in the background.
The arms of the starfish are tightly attached to the mussel's shell.

When a starfish regenerates all its other arms and body from a broken-off arm, it is called
a comet. This brightly colored, patterned starfish lives in the tropical waters off Hawaii.

Starfish don't eat or travel on their backs, so if one gets flipped over it must turn itself rightside up again.

Some starfish may throw off parts of their arms if they are disturbed. New arms will grow in about a year.

The starfish's mouth is in the middle of the underside of its body. With its arms it can pull at the shells of bivalves like clams and mussels. When a clam's shells open just the tiniest bit, the starfish pushes its stomach out of its mouth and into the bivalve. Now the stomach is inside out and can begin to digest the clam meat while outside of the starfish's body.

A starfish on algae at low tide on the New England coast

A candy cane starfish, common to the Indo-Pacific, seen here on a soft coral

A western Pacific starfish with slender arms. To its left are the scalloped edges of a giant clam.

Starfish lay their eggs in water. The eggs have developed inside of the starfish's arms and come out of tiny holes on the upper sides, near the bases of the arms.

You'll find starfish on the rocks or in the water of tide pools or in sandy puddles on the beach just about all over the world.

A red sun star on the coast of Maine. Large spines stick out from the edges of its arms.

Two brittle stars use their arms to pull themselves across the bottom of a tide pool in the Red Sea.

A spiny-armed brittle star that has ventured forth from its normal hideout in a rocky crevice in southern California waters

$Brittle$ $stars$ are similar to their cousins the starfish and get their name from the ease with which they break off arms. As with starfish, brittle star arms grow back. Their arms, however, are usually longer and more flexible than those of starfish, helping them to move faster. Sometimes the brittle star slithers along by stretching an arm forward, fixing the tip of it to a surface, then pulling its body forward by wriggling and bending the stretched-out arm. The brittle star can also crawl about in two other ways. One arm can lead, two can trail behind, and the two in between can move in a

Brittle stars may use their flexible arms to hold onto sponges, corals, and other animals.

rowing or pushing motion. Or four arms can row and the fifth will trail behind.

The tube feet on a brittle star's arms usually don't have suction cups. They are used to breathe, to feel around, and to "sniff" out the small living and dead animals that brittle stars like to eat.

You can find brittle stars in all the oceans of the world. Some live in deep water and some in shallow water, including tide pools. You'll never find brittle stars on the rocks above the water, though. They need to be in water all the time.

A short-spined brittle star from western Mexico. Many brittle stars are most active at night. They spend the day hidden away in dark crevices.

If you look closely, you will see sea urchins inside these holes they have burrowed into rock on the shore of a Caribbean island.

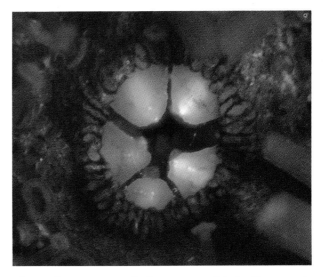

An enlargement of the sea urchin's five teeth. These are used for scraping, pulling, and tearing algae off hard surfaces. The teeth continue to grow throughout the urchin's life, so they are never worn down completely.

$\mathcal{T}$he colorful, prickly sea urchin can anchor itself to rocks with its spines and tube feet so that the waves won't wash it away. As it holds on tight, it gnaws part of the rock away with its teeth. The sea urchin's mouth, located on the underside of its body, has five powerful white teeth and looks so much like an ancient Greek oil lantern that it has been called "Aristotle's Lantern."

This relative of the starfish and brittle star is covered with spines. The spines help the urchin move around or turn upright again after it has been flipped over, and some urchins have spines that sting as well.

Sea urchins usually eat seaweed, but they also eat bits of other plants and animals. Some are called sea eggs because of the shape of their bodies.

The long, sharp spines of this Caribbean sea urchin are dangerous to skin divers. The thing that looks like a pearl amidst this urchin's spines is its rectum, which is sometimes pushed outside of its body.

Two small urchins from the coast of New England. Urchins can graze algae so close that the rocks look almost bare.

Slate pencil urchins, like this one in Hawaii, are also common to waters off northern Australia, Indonesia, Malaysia, and the Philippines. The heavy spines probably help defend the urchin.

A pencil urchin from Florida. The widely spaced, large spines of this urchin are each surrounded by smaller spines.

A dead sand dollar washed up on a beach

The sand dollar's short spines act like tiny shovels to help it burrow in the sand. Its tube feet are located in the star shape and are used like gills for breathing.

One of the nicest souvenirs of a day at the beach is a sand dollar. The sand dollar is a type of sea urchin. It's a flat, circle-shaped creature that looks a little like a silver dollar made of sand.

You may find sand dollars on the sandy bottom of a tide pool or in the ocean itself. When alive, most sand dollars have tube feet and short, bristling spines which help them burrow in the sand.

When a sand dollar dies, it loses its bristles and tube feet and feels like sandpaper to the touch. You can find shells of dead sand dollars on the beach.

A North Atlantic sand dollar with periwinkles

An upside-down sand dollar. Its mouth is at the center of the disc.

When is a cucumber not a cucumber? When it's a sea cucumber, of course. These cousins of the starfish are animals.

Sea cucumbers live in all oceans in either deep or shallow water or in tide pools. They usually range in length from 2 to 18 inches (5 to 45 cm), but some are under 1 inch (2.5 cm) and others have been measured at 3 feet (90 cm) and longer.

The front end of a worm-like sea cucumber showing its tentacles extended. The sticky tentacles surround the cucumber's mouth and are used for dabbing up particles of food.

The rear end of a sea cucumber showing its anus. The sea cucumber excretes waste through its anus and can also breathe through it by pumping water in and out.

If the water gets very shallow, some cucumbers can curl up into a ball to protect themselves from being dried out by the sun. When the water returns, the cucumber relaxes, stretches out, and shows off the ring of tentacles around its mouth. Sometimes the cucumber dries out in the process of stretching. Then it looks like a brittle piece of seaweed. But the tidewater will revive it.

Sea cucumbers often burrow in the wet sand. They swallow a lot of sand in the process, digesting the organic material (bits of other animals and plants), and eliminating the rest. In this way they act very much as earthworms do on land.

Blue sponges near Acapulco, Mexico. Water is taken into the sponge's body through many tiny pores and let out through the large openings. This is an encrusting sponge. It grows by spreading over the surface of the rock.

This red finger sponge from the Red Sea grows in the form of slender branches.

Yellow finger sponge in Boston harbor. Sponges grow in many shapes. Most other animals do not.

$\mathcal{M}$*ost household sponges* are manufactured from synthetic materials, but *some* household sponges were once animals. Only certain animal sponges can become household sponges, though. Many are too prickly.

Saltwater sponges are animals filled with holes and channels. They have no heads, mouths, stomachs, or any other internal organs. Water flows right through them. Sponges take their food from this flowing water.

Finger sponge in New England waters. Upright forms like this are more often found in deeper waters. Encrusting sponges grow closer to the shore.

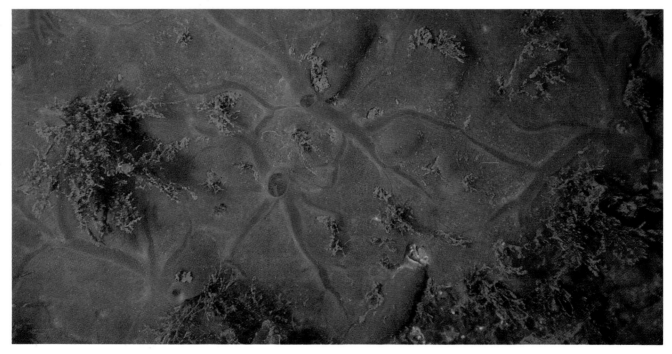

A red encrusting sponge in the Mediterranean Sea. You can see the canals that gather water from within the body before it is pumped out.

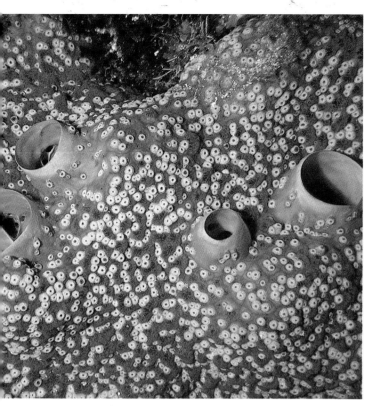

This red sponge on the Caribbean coast of Mexico is covered with small white sea anemones growing on its body.

Sponges 1 to 4 inches (2.5 to 10 cm) tall can live on the floors and sides of tide pools. You'll find much larger sponges living farther out in the ocean, but the sponges in shallow water are often more colorful, and in the tropics those colors may be even more intense.

You'll find sponges all over the world, but natural household sponges come mostly from the eastern half of the Mediterranean and waters near Mexico and the Bahamas.

Upright sponges can be found all around the world. This pink one is on the Caribbean coast of Mexico. Notice the brittle star's arm at the top of the sponge. Sponges provide homes for many kinds of animals.

These North Atlantic sea squirts are called sea peaches because they look like the fruit.

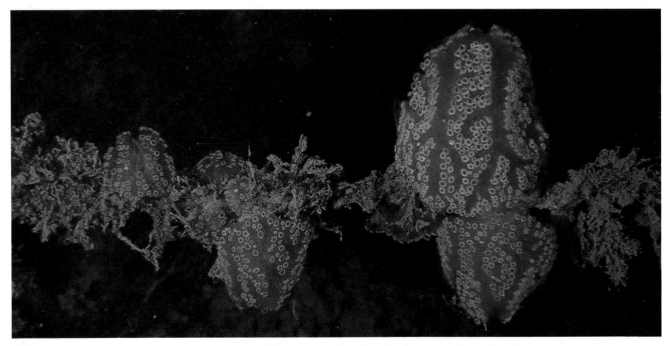

Colonies of sea squirts growing on an old rope in the Mediterranean Sea. Colonial sea squirts group together in a jelly-like mass. Each tiny white circle is the tip of one siphon.

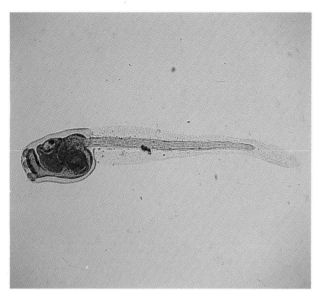

A sea squirt seen in its "tadpole" stage, magnified through a microscope

Do sea squirts squirt? Touch one and find out! It just might spray you with a stream of water. The sea squirt contracts when it is disturbed and sends out a spray of water through one of its tubes, called siphons. These siphons are more often used to obtain food and eliminate waste. The sea squirt draws in water through one of its two siphons, strains it across gill slits where organic food is trapped, and lets the rest out through its other siphon.

When the sea squirt hatches from its egg, it looks a lot like a tadpole. It has a tail and swims freely. But it changes shape as it grows. An adult looks like a plump bag with two tubes coming out of it. It no longer swims. Instead it stays in one place, attached to seaweed, rocks, or wharf pilings.

Scientists call sea squirts *chordates* because of the tadpole-like stage in their early growth. Humans are chordates also. We, too, looked like tadpoles for a short time before we were born.

Sea squirts can be found all over the world, sometimes attached to the bottoms of ships, but most prefer shallow water.

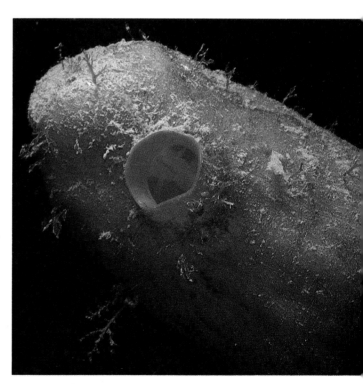

Looking inside one of a sea squirt's siphons, we can see the chamber in which its gill filters food and oxygen from the water.

This clam, called a cockle shell, has its foot extended. The tissue on the inside edges of its shells is called the mantle. As the clam grows, the mantle will secrete new shell.

Giant clams, found in the East Indies and off the Australian coast, can grow to lengths of 4 feet (120 cm) and weights of 500 pounds (230 kilograms).

You'll find clams on the bottom of the ocean in either shallow or deep water or buried in the sand along the beach when the tide is out. Clams are bivalves, as are oysters, mussels, and scallops. Bivalves are creatures that have two shells hinged together in one place. Different varieties of clams live all over the world.

Water enters and leaves the clam's shells through a pair of tubes called siphons. The siphons stick out of the shells when the water around the clam is high. Water and food particles of plants and animals can then flow into the clam. But when the tide is out or at any time the clam senses danger, it pulls in its siphons—and its foot—and fastens its shells tightly closed. This is where we get the expression "clamming up."

A clam's foot can extend downward through the open shells. The clam is able to dig deeply into sand or mud with this foot. In this way it can hide from creatures that might want to turn it into a meal.

Clams are burrowing animals. Their cousins the scallops are swimmers.
Unlike most clams, scallops have many small blue eyes on the edges of their mantles.

File shell clams, such as this one on the Florida coast, are found in tropical waters.
This file shell has well-developed tentacles that help make it aware of changes in the water around it.

A *hermit crab* lives in the empty shell of a dead snail. It will take over the shell of a dead snail, or it may drag a dying snail out of its shell and have the snail for lunch before making itself at home.

The hermit steals shells for homes because, unlike other crabs, it has soft, unprotected rear parts. It forms its soft body to the spiral inside the snail shell, and when threatened it can draw itself entirely inside, using its tough claws like a door to seal the shell's opening.

Hermit crabs are found in oceans and on beaches all over the world. During low tide, you can find them on the floors of tide pools. Others cluster together on the ocean floor. Still others live on land, and some of these even climb into trees.

A tropical green spotted hermit crab tucked into a textile cone shell. The snail that used to live in this shell is extremely poisonous.

Two hermit crabs in shells to fit. The large hermit crab has extended its two claws and walking legs. The small one has pulled into its shell and plugged the opening with its two claws.

A hermit crab outside of its shell. Notice its soft, coiled abdomen. As the hermit crab grows, it will have to replace its old shell with a larger one.

Moon jellies catch most of their food on long, frilly arms that hang down around their mouths.

This jellyfish, from the coast of Washington state, traps its food with long tentacles on the edge of its bell-shaped body.

If you walk along the beach, you may sometime see a jelly-like mass. Probably it's a jellyfish.

A jellyfish has a fragile inner and outer body wall. Contained between these two walls is the jelly-like material that makes up this animal's soft skeleton and gives it its name.

A jellyfish swims by opening its body like an umbrella, then quickly closing it again, thus pushing water out from underneath its body. This rapidly re-peated action, or jet propulsion, pushes the animal upward or forward. When it stops swimming, it begins to sink, catching the tiny animals that it dines

Moon jellies can be found in temperate and tropical waters around the world.

on as it comes down on top of them.

Jellyfish can sting, and because of this some jellyfish are very dangerous. One kind, called the sea wasp, has a poison more deadly than that of any poisonous snake. Sea wasps live in coastal waters near northern Australia and the Philippines.

Many jellyfish prefer warm, tropical waters, but you can also find jellyfish on British and American shores. The jellyfish you see washed up on the shore most likely have died. However they should not be handled because some can still sting.

This large jellyfish washed up on a California beach after a storm. Sometimes jellyfish get trapped in tide pools.

A red alga growing in southern California

One of the most common sights at the shore is seaweed. Most of the common saltwater plants we know as seaweed are kinds of algae. The tide brings them to shore.

Seaweed is very important to sea creatures. Many animals find shelter from the sun by hiding in patches of it. Some take on the color of the seaweed and so are well hidden from attackers. Other animals feed on seaweed.

A Moroccan girl sits next to a freshly collected bale of red algae. (Algae is the plural of alga.)

Seaweed can be useful to people too. We get iodine from kelp, a brown seaweed, as well as a substance called algin. Algin is used in making ice cream. It keeps the water in the milk from making ice crystals when the ice cream is frozen. You can also find algin in salad dressings, chocolate milk, and aspirin.

A red seaweed called Irish Moss or carrageen comes from Ireland, France, New England, and Canada. It's used in soups, desserts, and jams.

The Japanese prepare seaweed to eat by itself. This food, called nori, is usually made with a red seaweed that helps digestion.

Kelp forests like this one grow along the California coast. The kelp provides shelter for many kinds of animals.

If you have been to an ocean, you know how big and exciting it is. Maybe you have collected shells washed onto the shore and met some tide pool animals already. If you haven't been to an ocean yet, a wonderful experience is waiting for you.

Close your eyes. Imagine a steady, rolling sound. Pretend your feet are bare and there is a slightly salty taste on your lips. The wind is blowing your hair, the water is cooling your toes, and the sun is keeping you warm. This is the place where the waves break. *Welcome.*

About Scientific Classification

Are elephants, skunks, and sea cucumbers all in the same scientific group? You bet! They all belong in the "Animal Kingdom," one of the largest groups. This keeps them separate from petunias, oak trees, and seaweeds, all of which belong in the "Plant Kingdom," another of the largest groups. These kingdoms are the first and largest groups in a system known as "scientific classification."

In all, scientific classification includes seven chief groups. These are, from the largest to the smallest: (1) kingdom, (2) phylum, (3) class, (4) order, (5) family, (6) genus, and (7) species. A kingdom has many very different kinds of members in it. In a phylum, the members all become more alike, and so on down to the species, in which the members are all very much alike.

The following classifications show some of the larger scientific groups within which all the animals and plants in this book belong. These words may seem strange at first because, like all scientific names, they are either Greek or Latin. This is so that scientists all over the world, whether they speak Chinese, English, or Arabic, can understand the same word for a plant or animal.

Animal Kingdom

Snail: Phylum: Mollusca
Class: Gastropoda

Periwinkle: Phylum: Mollusca
Class: Gastropoda
Family: Littorinidae

Starfish: Phylum: Echinodermata
Class: Asteroidea

Brittle Star:	Phylum: Echinodermata
	Class: Ophiuroidea
Sea Urchin:	Phylum: Echinodermata
	Class: Echinoidea
Sand Dollar:	Phylum: Echinodermata
	Class: Echinoidea
Sea Cucumber:	Phylum: Echinodermata
	Class: Holothuroidea
Sponge:	Phylum: Porifera
Sea Squirt:	Phylum: Chordata
	Class: Ascidiacea
Clam:	Phylum: Mollusca
	Class: Bivalvia
Hermit Crab:	Phylum: Arthropoda
	Class: Crustacea
	Family: Paguridae
Jellyfish:	Phylum: Cnidaria
	Class: Scyphozoa

Plant Kingdom

Seaweed:

Green Alga:	Phylum: Chlorophyta
Brown Alga:	Phylum: Phaeophyta
Red Alga:	Phylum: Rhodophyta

Index